Michelle Cole

S

COVID-19

N

COVID-19

Copyright © 2020 Michelle Cole

Scripture quotations are from the Holy Bible (King James version).

All other quotes are from Michelle Cole.

Write World Publishing Group
3839 McKinney Avenue
Suite: 155-373
Dallas, TX 75204

Writeworld@cs.com

Author Contact: info@MichelleCole.org

ISBN: 978-0-9722173-6-1

Write World
"we write the books that make the whole world read!"®

THANK YOUS

First and foremost, I thank God, who makes all things possible! I also thank Him for giving me insight to write this book.

A **special thank you to my beautiful** mother, Lillie Mae Cole, "**Mommie**," who has always loved and supported me, since birth.

Thank you to all essential workers, frontline workers and first responders. Your hard work and dedication are greatly appreciated.

Books by Michelle Cole:

LILLA BELLE THE FIRST STAGES

F.A.T. CHANCE

CANCER, MEET THE CURE!

VENGEANCE (**Upcoming Thriller)

*****

We have never seen anything quite like the coronavirus disease 2019 (COVID-19) in the 21st century. God brought His world to a standstill. He interrupted business as usual. He has changed life as we know it. COVID-19 turned the world upside down.

Contrary to beliefs, man doesn't rule the world; the One who created it does. When we reject God and become lifted up in pride, God knows how to bring us down to size. He knows how to put us back in our place. Is it a coincidence that many of the things that we love doing were temporarily shut down and off limits to us? The One True God temporarily removed our gods. **Christ *is* in this crisis.** Will we take heed to God's global warning?

"Who can speak and have it happen if the Lord has not decreed it? Is it not from the mouth of the Most High that both calamities and good things come?" (Lamentations 3:37-38)

God brought the world to a standstill. He interrupted business as usual. He has changed life as we know it. The coronavirus disease 2019 (COVID-19) turned the world upside down. Cities, towns and entire countries were shut down. Churches, schools and countless businesses shut their doors in every corner of the world. Streets were empty. The sports world has been put on hold. And once-crowded airports were practically empty. This deadly virus, which reportedly originated in Wuhan, China, in December of 2019, is a global pandemic.

To date, there are more than 14,700,000 COVID-19 confirmed cases, globally, and more than 610,000 deaths. In the United States, there are more than 4,000,000 confirmed cases and more than 142,000 deaths. And counting. Many of our hospitals are at full capacity and some are at breaking point. Doctors and nurses are working around the clock and some have lost their lives while trying to save lives. Other essential workers and first responders have also lost their lives. Personal protective equipment (PPE) continues to be a major issue in our hospitals. Testing and contact tracing are also major issues. Suicide, domestic violence and substance abuse are on the rise. More than 40 million Americans have lost their jobs. Unemployment is at an all-time high. Thousands wait in miles-long lines as food banks struggle to keep up with demand. The once-thriving economy has quickly collapsed. Scientists are working hard to find a vaccine, however, there is currently no cure.

Looking for face masks? Hand sanitizer? Lysol? Disposable gloves? How about Clorox wipes? The fear and panic of shortages quickly wipe out store shelves as soon as shelves are stocked with these supplies. And like the rest of the world, manufacturers are struggling to keep up with the high demand.

"Stay at home" and "social distancing" (stay 6 feet apart when you go out in public) are familiar phrases. Physical distancing is a better term. Wash your hands, often, for at least 20 seconds. Wear a face mask when going out in public. In addition to a face mask, I also wear disposable gloves whenever I leave home. Wearing a face mask is crucial; I would much rather wear a face mask than a ventilator.

*****

After weeks of sheltering-in-place, most states started loosening restrictions in May. However, more than half of the states reopened without meeting the guidelines that were recommended by the Center for Disease Control and Prevention (CDC). And as a result, COVID-19 cases have surged to new highs – yet again. We must all do our part to help slow the spread of this deadly pandemic.

We have lived through numerous wars and other disasters before: earthquakes, hurricanes, Ebola, Katrina and 9/11, but we have never seen or experienced anything quite like COVID-19 in the 21st century. I have never seen anything like this in my lifetime. And chances are, you haven't either.

*****

Since mid-March, the world has expressed feelings of: panic, fear, despair, confusion, anger and sadness. For some, COVID-19 is like a horror movie. For others, a nightmare.

*****

The world was brought to its knees by the One who created the world – God. The most powerful and the richest nation in the world, the United States, has been unable to deal with this global crisis. New York City, the largest city in America, looked like a ghost town. As did the immensely-popular Las Vegas Strip. This invisible and deadly virus, this global pandemic, has wreaked havoc, and it is still wreaking havoc, throughout the world. How do we fight something that we cannot see? And *why* did this happen?

First and foremost, we need to turn to the One who *can* see all things – God. Not only has COVID-19 plagued our land, an even deadlier virus is also plaguing our land – sin. If all we see is that we need to get back to work. We need to get out of the house. We need to get back to business as usual; we will miss the wake-up call from God.

The world needs a spiritual awakening. A revival. We need to take heed to what God is saying to us. Why did God temporarily shut down His world? Why did He bring things to a temporary standstill? I said "His" for a reason. This is God's world. We just live in it.

*****

COVID-19 is shaking the world. And it is, God, who is doing the shaking. COVID-19 is about sin. It is a wake-up call for us to repent and turn to God. It is a divine disruption. I use "we" and "us" throughout this book, due to the fact that we have all sinned and fallen short of the glory of God.

During these very unprecedented times, the gospel song, "If We Ever Needed the Lord Before," (We Sure Do Need Him Now), comes to mind.

This global pandemic may have taken us by surprise, however, it did not take God by surprise. Nothing catches Him off guard. When bad things happen, we often ask, "Where are You, God?" He is right where He has always been. The Scripture tells us where He is. "God reigns over the nations; God is seated on His holy throne" (Psalm 47:8). He does not appear during good times and then disappear in bad times. He is ever-present.

God has unique attributes that belong only to Him. He is omnipotent – which means that He is all-powerful. There is nothing that He cannot do. His power is limitless. And unmatched. "I know that You can do all things," Job says in his own repentance, "and that no purpose of Yours can be thwarted" (Job 42:2). "Who can speak and have it happen if the Lord has not decreed it? Is it not from the mouth of the Most High that both calamities and good things come?" (Lamentations 3:37-38)

God is omniscient – which means that He is all-knowing. One sparrow will not fall to the ground without God knowing about it. The very hairs on our heads are all numbered. He knows what we are going to say before we even say it. "Before a word is on my tongue You know it completely, O Lord" (Psalm 139:4).

There is nothing hidden from God. He sees the past, present and future, simultaneously. "I make known the end from the beginning, from ancient times, what is still to come. I say, My purpose will stand, and I will do all that I please" (Isaiah 46:10). "I am Alpha and the Omega, the First and the Last, the Beginning and the End" (Revelation 22:13). "From heaven the Lord looks down and sees all mankind; from His dwelling place. He watches all who live on earth. He who forms the hearts of all, who considers everything they do" (Psalm 33:13-15).

Almighty God is all-seeing and all-knowing. He knows what's going to happen before it even takes place. In full detail. He also has the power to stop anything if He chooses to do so. Unlike man, God doesn't think that He knows it all. He *does* know it all.

God is omnipresent – which means that He is present everywhere. "Can a man hide himself in secret places so that I cannot see him?" saith the Lord. "Do I not fill heaven and earth?" saith the Lord. (Jeremiah 23:24)

God is also sovereign; which means that He, and He alone, is in control of all things. There is nothing that is out of His control. His will and purpose will always stand. Nothing happens by luck, fate, or chance. Nothing. "I form the light, and create darkness: I make peace and create evil: I, the Lord do all these things" (Isaiah 45:7).

In order to understand life, and its many uncertainties, we must understand God's sovereignty. COVID-19 is a reminder that we are not in control. It also reminds us that life is uncertain. Tomorrow is not promised. God is always in control even when things look like they are out of control. We may panic; but God never does.

It is interesting how we seem to think that we are in control until something happens that reminds us that we are not. The truth is, we are not in control, we were never in control and we will never be in control – of anything. Our trust should always be in the One who is in control of all things – God.

Oftentimes, suffering highlights what is most important to us – family and basic necessities. When our world is shaken, we often turn to God. This global pandemic has also brought many of us to our knees. People who have never prayed before are now praying. More and more people are also turning to God. Some who turned away from God are now turning back to Him. These are indeed very frightening times, however, God's people shouldn't be frightened. "For God hath not given us the spirit of fear; but of power, and of love, and of a sound mind" (2 Timothy 1:7). "Who of you by worrying can add a single hour to his life?" (Matthew 6:27) God does not want us to worry or to be fearful. Instead, He wants us to trust Him. Because after all, all things are in God's hands.

*****

COVID-19 is what happens when we depart from God. Declaring independence from Him was one of our biggest mistakes. Contrary to beliefs, we are not self-sufficient. Nor are we independent. We are all dependent on God. He is independent of us, however, we are not independent of Him, nor will we ever be. Apart from God, we can do nothing.

God has unsurpassed love for us. Where would we be without His love, mercy and grace? Where would we be without Him, period? God is loving and forgiving. But there is also another side of God – His wrath. "But the Lord is the true God; He is the living God, the eternal King. When He is angry, the Earth trembles; the nations cannot endure His wrath" (Jeremiah 10:10). "For the wrath of God is revealed from heaven against all ungodliness and unrighteousness of men, who by their unrighteousness suppress the truth" (Romans 1:18).

In this very secular world, we have created God in our own image and after our own likeness. There are also countless sermons that God is love and only love. The Bible, God's Word, is clear. God hates sin and He will judge all who have not repented and trusted in His Son, Jesus Christ.

Almighty God is holy. "Because it is written, Be ye holy; for I Am holy" (1 Peter 1:16). Sin separates us from God. Jesus died on the cross for our sins. He paid our sin debt — in full. On the third day, He rose from the grave with all power, in heaven and in earth, in His hands. Jesus said to her, "I Am the Resurrection and the Life. Whoever believes in Me, though he die, yet shall he live" (John 11:25). "I and the Father are One" (John 10:30).

This world is full of sin. And it's not getting any better. In fact, it is getting worse and worse. Sin is plaguing our land like never before: idolatry, adultery, murder, sexual immorality, theft, violence … When we reject God, we are headed for destruction — hence, COVID-19.

*****

We are very arrogant and prideful; at least some of us are. When we try to exalt ourselves, God will bring us down. However, when we humble ourselves, God will raise us up. "Humble yourselves before the Lord, and He will exalt you" (James 4:10).

Pride is a way of saying that we don't need God. We are all God-dependent. We are not self-dependent or independent. Many of us have heard the term, "self-made man." That's not a myth; it is a lie. Not only did God create us, it is He who sustains us; every second, every minute, every hour and every day of our lives. Who keeps our hearts beating? We are all on His ventilator. We are all in God's hands.

To think that we are independent, smarter and wiser than God is very foolish. Pride is synonymous in Scripture with arrogance, evil, wickedness, foolishness and scoffing. It is the opposite of what pleases God – people who are God-fearing, humble and meek. "To fear the Lord is to hate evil; I hate pride and arrogance, evil behavior and perverse speech" (Proverbs 8:13). When we are prideful, instead of depending on the God who created us, we decide what is good and what is evil; when in fact, God, our Creator, has already decided that. God already decided what sin is.

God's standards were set before He created this world. And His Word and standards are not up for debate. Even in the 21st century. "Whoever has a haughty look and an arrogant heart I will not endure" (Psalm 101:5). "The wicked, through the pride of his countenance, will not seek after God: God is not in all his thoughts" (Psalm 10:4). How can we be independent of the One who created us? It is not possible. How can we possibly think that we are wiser than the All-Knowing and All-Powerful God? How can we possibly think that we are in control? How can we possibly think that we don't need God? It is He who decides if we will take our very next breath.

*****

In addition to being very prideful, we can also add very foolish to that list. "The fool hath said in his heart, there is no God. They are corrupt, they have done abominable works, there is none that doeth good" (Psalm 14:1).

We exist to rely on God. To glorify Him. And worship Him; in spirit and in truth. "God *is* Spirit, and those who worship Him must worship in spirit and truth" (John 4:24).

The deeper our worship, the more that God is glorified. And the more that we know God, the more we will trust Him.

God is a jealous God. He will not be in competition with anyone. Or anything. "Do not worship any other god, for the Lord, whose name is Jealous, is a jealous God" (Exodus 34:14). In addition to pride, there are countless gods (idols) in today's world: money, material things, celebrity worshipping, our careers, our spouses, our significant others ... God must be first in our lives. He is second to none. He takes a backseat to no one and no thing. Anything, or anyone, that we put before God – is an idol. It is a god. When we do this, the One and Only True God – is not pleased. "Thou shalt have no other gods before Me" (Exodus 20:3). God punished Israel, numerous times, throughout the Bible, for worshipping other gods. COVID-19 is a reminder of who God is and what He will not tolerate. "Who *is* like You, O Lord, among the gods? Who *is* like You, glorious in holiness, fearful in praises, doing wonders?" (Exodus 15:11)

*****

Before this global pandemic, some often bragged about "our" great economy. Some politicians even stated that they were the reason for the great economy. Some said that it was because of our current president. Or a former president. I have some news for you, if the economy was great because of man, any man, that includes any president, past or present, it would still be great. Instead of bragging, we should have been thanking the One who made it great – God. The economy that man took credit for has quickly collapsed. We are now experiencing economic devastation. A decade of job gains was wiped out in one single month. How many of us thanked God when the economy was great? How many of us gave Him credit? I often hear people say that God works slowly.

Not so. No one can put God in a box. As the Scriptures tell us, God does whatever He pleases. And He works however He wants to work. Slowly or at lightning speed; it is God's choice. There was nothing slow about COVID-19. This deadly, invisible virus moved swiftly throughout the world. And, likewise, the once-great economy, was decimated – quickly. Only God can do what is being done. He showed that He is all-powerful. He is mighty. And we are powerless. Will God stop this virus and restore the economy? Possibly. However, it is very important that we take heed to this wake-up call. The last thing we need to do is become more arrogant. We need to humble ourselves, repent and turn to God.

*****

Is it a coincidence that many of the things that we love doing were temporarily shut down and off limits to us? Traveling, going shopping, going to the movies, attending ball games, going to concerts, dining in restaurants, going to the nail shop, going to the beauty salon, barber shop … The One True God temporarily removed our gods.

We will never be perfect, however, that should never stop us from improving – especially spiritually. Some are obsessed with their outward appearance, but God looks at the heart. We all have work to do. Some more than others.

*****

We don't have time for God. Do we have time for Him now? We don't want God in our lives. We don't want Him in society. We don't want Him in our homes, in our courts, on our jobs, or in our schools ... The irony is we don't have anything without Him. That includes the most important thing of all that we often take for granted – life. The very breath that we breathe – comes from God. Please let that marinate for a moment.

*****

Contrary to beliefs, man doesn't rule the world. The One who created it does. God is not just the Creator of this world, He is the Creator of all things; that includes – all human beings. Animals, birds, you name it. We belong to Him. "The earth is the Lord's and the fullness thereof, the world and they that dwell therein" (Psalm 24). When we reject God and become lifted up in pride, God knows how to bring us back down to size. He knows how to put us back in our place. "Pride goeth before destruction and a haughty spirit before a fall" (Proverbs 16:18). COVID-19 has made many nations fall, including the mightiest nation of all – the United States of America. It is actually "His" United States of America. And we would all do well to remember that.

*****

Anyone who knows me knows how much I *love* Christmas! It is, by far, my favorite holiday. Some of us have also tried to remove Christ out of Christmas; "write X-mas instead." And some employers don't want employees saying, "Merry Christmas." However, it is okay to say, "Happy Holidays." Any wonder why we are experiencing the most devastating pestilence in the 21st century? Christ will never be removed, but He can certainly remove us.

＊＊＊＊＊

We seem to ignore God when things are going well; but the moment something bad happens, we turn to Him, sometimes angrily, with questions: "Where are You, God?" "Why is this happening?" "Why do bad things happen to good people?" "Why won't You stop this?" We answer to God. He does not answer to us. Sometimes God answers our questions and sometimes He doesn't. Almighty God does not have to explain anything to us. Nor does He owe us anything. There are many things in life that we will never be able to understand. However, God does tell us to trust Him. Even if or when we don't understand. Even if or when we may not agree; we still need to trust Him. God doesn't just see the big picture; He sees the whole picture. And He knows exactly how it is going to end. "For My thoughts are not your thoughts, neither are your ways My ways" declares the Lord. "As the heavens are higher than the earth, so are My ways higher than your ways and My thoughts than your thoughts" (Isaiah 55:8).

＊＊＊＊＊

God is not a spare tire. There are many "spare-tire Christians." When there is an emergency we turn to God. When we hit rock bottom – we turn to God. He is not a "just-in-case God." Nor is He a last-resort God. God should always be first in our lives. We need Him in good times as well as bad times. "But if You turn away from them, they panic. You take away their breath, they die and turn again to dust. When You give them Your breath, life is created, and You renew the face of the earth"

(Psalm 104:29-30). God controls all things. He is Lord over all. That includes life and death. "See now that I, even I, am He, and there is no god besides Me. I kill, and I make alive; I wound, and I heal; neither is there any that can deliver out of My hand" (Deuteronomy 32:39). We know our birthdates, however, only God knows when we will take our last breath. "Let everything that hath breath praise ye the Lord" (Psalm 150:6). I often say, "God knows it all, owns it all and controls it all. If all we have is God; we have more than enough!"

*****

A pestilence (plague) is a part of God's judgment — against sin. Sometimes God also sends pestilences to unbelievers. God does not change. "Jesus Christ is the same yesterday, today and forevermore" (Hebrews 13:8).

In the Bible, there were numerous pestilences sent by God. Some are listed below:

- God sent 10 plagues upon the Egyptians before the Israelites left Egypt (Exodus 7:14-12:36).
- God promised judgment if the people of Israel turned against Him. Part of God's judgment included plagues (Leviticus 26:25).
- God sent a 3-day plague to wipe out 70,000 men after David sinned by numbering the people of Israel (2 Samuel 24:10–17).
- Amos prophesied that God would send several judgments against the nation of Israel, including plagues similar to what Egypt had endured (Amos 4:10).

- ○ God sent several judgments against the nation of Judah, including a plague, when he sent King Nebuchadnezzar to sack Jerusalem (Jeremiah 21:7, 24:10, 29:17).
- ○ The plagues described in the Book of Revelation, including those sent by the two witnesses, (Revelation 11:6) and the 7 final plagues sent by God (Revelation 15:1).

The most devastating pestilence thus far of the 21st century, COVID-19, can now be added to the list. Sodom and Gomorrah also serve as a lesson of the consequences of sin and the wrath of God. As does the flood; (how God destroyed the world the first time). The biggest judgment is yet to come. COVID-19 is a wakeup call. And what a wake-up call it is!

$$*****$$

How are our churches doing today? From the looks of things, our churches have a lot of work to do. They are in trouble. Instead of being salt and light to the world, churches seem to be emulating the world. Churches are looking and acting more and more secular. Christians should be examples for sinners, examples for the world. The blind cannot lead the blind. 'Then Jesus gave the following illustration: "Can one blind person lead another? Won't they both fall into a ditch?" (Luke 6:39) Church leaders, are you leading by the example set by Christ? Anyone leading a double life? How are we living our lives when we're not in church? When we think no one is watching. Please know that the One and Only, All-Seeing God, sees and knows all. There is nothing hidden from Him. How many of us wouldn't have a prayer life if we didn't have problems?

Church has become big business. David was a man after God's own heart. How many pastors seek money, fame and material wealth? How many are passionate about Jesus? Worshipping Him? Glorifying Him? What about leading others to Christ?

Name it and claim it. Prosperity gospel. Give money and get a blessing from God? God is not a bank or ATM machine. We don't need to give God money in order for Him to bless us. God doesn't need our money; He owns it all. "Who has given to Me that I should repay him? Everything under heaven is Mine" (Job 41:11). God already knows what we need before we even ask Him. God can also bless us in countless ways, not just financially. I experienced my first big blessing this morning — God woke me up!

The church is the Body of Christ. God's Word and standards should never be compromised. Some churches today try to be all things to all people. Some church leaders are afraid to speak out against sin for fear of losing members and donations. Some care more about being politically-correct than Christ-correct. "If favor is shown to the wicked, he does not learn righteousness; in the land of uprightness he deals corruptly and does not see the majesty of the Lord" (Isaiah 26:10).

Some churches have little reverence for God. Some pastors seem to take pride in the fact that, "our church doesn't feel like church." What exactly does that mean? How can there be church, without God? Without His Word? Without His principles? A church without God is in big trouble. A school without God is in big trouble. A world without God is in big trouble. Every human being without God is in big trouble. It is very foolish to think that we are better off without our Creator.

Church attendance was down sharply before COVID-19. More than likely, there will be a sharp rise in church attendance when churches reopen their doors. But how long will it last? We make time for everything else; we also need to make time for God. It is important to go to church, pray regularly and have an intimate relationship with God. Knowing about God is not sufficient. We need to know Him. There is a big difference between the two.

When there are sick people in our communities, where is the church? Where are the pastors? The deacons? Do church members visit the sick? What about calling the sick and praying with them over the phone? What about seeing if they need anything? Giving is not always about money. We can give our time. Take them food. Run errands for them ... We can let them know that they are in our thoughts and prayers. Christians, it is biblically-commanded that we care for one another, specifically those who are sick.

God is also a healer. How many of you were sick and then healed by God? Did you thank Him for healing you? When God healed me of cancer, I thanked Him. And 22 years later, I still thank Him. I appreciate doctors, nurses and modern medicine, but it is God (Jehovah-Rapha) who heals.

*****

How are today's schools doing? Have our schools become better or worse – without prayer? We went from beginning each school day publicly praying to not praying at all. The Supreme Court declared school-sponsored prayer and Bible readings – unconstitutional. As a result, there has been a rapid moral decline in America's schools. Over the years, the absence of school prayer has been linked to almost every social ill, from school shootings to drug addiction.

School prayer was removed from schools, but false teachings are allowed? Some schools are teaching students that human beings came from monkeys. That is a lie. If anyone wants to know how we came into being, they need only to reach for the nearest Bible. It is all there. "God created man in His own image, in the image of God, He created them; male and female He created them" (Genesis 1:27). In addition, that same God also created monkeys. He is the Creator of all things.

*****

"Is homosexuality a sin?" I watched as a pastor struggled with this question. No pun intended, but he never gave a straight answer. When, or if, we want to know the answer to this question, or if we want to know the answer to any question, we just need to reach for the nearest Bible. The answer to this question is, "yes," homosexuality *is* a sin. It is an abomination. I didn't say it, God said it. His Word is clear. "You shall not lie with a male as with a woman; it is an abomination" (Leviticus 18:22). All teaching must align itself with the Bible. Does God love people who are homosexual? He absolutely does! I am sure that many of you have heard this before – God loves sinners, however, He hates sin.

No one can overrule what God has already ruled on. God decides what the standards are. For marriage. And for all things life. And He has already decided. "In the beginning was the Word, and the Word was with God, and the Word was God" (John 1:1).

Who are we to approve what God has disapproved? For this reason a man will leave his father and mother and be united to his wife, and the two will become one flesh" (Ephesians 5:31).

Before man was created, before we even knew what a Supreme Court was, God's standards were set. Who are we to redefine what God has already defined? The Supreme Court justices are not God. Nor is the Constitution the Bible. Most are familiar with the question, "who came first, the chicken or the egg?" Some have trouble answering that one. However, there is no doubt that the Bible came before the Constitution. The Constitution is man-made. The Bible is God's Word. God, the Creator of Man. Perfect in wisdom and knowledge. There is no comparison.

Nothing will ever trump God's Word. The Bible is our guide. It is what God gave us to live by. It is our reference guide. Our life guide. There is no expiration date on God's Word. Nor will there ever be. God will not be in competition with the Supreme Court or anyone. It is He who reigns supreme. And He alone. "Heaven and earth will pass away, but My words will never pass away" (Matthew 24:35).

*****

Climate change and global warming. Neither exists. Reportedly, 97% of climate scientists believe in climate change and global warming. The other 3% may be Christians. In addition to climate scientists, more and more people are saying that human activity is changing the climate — hence climate change and global warming. The only climate that we might be able to change is the climate in our homes and cars. No one can change anything that God, and God alone, created. God not only created the earth, He also sustains it. God didn't need our help when He created the earth; and He certainly doesn't need our help now. It brings to mind when God questioned Job. "Where were you when I laid the foundation of the earth? Tell Me, if you have understanding. Who determined its measurements — surely you know! Or who stretched the line upon it?" (Job 38-42) Please note, I did not include all of the Bible verses, however, please read all of Job 38-42.

*****

Scientists will never be ahead of God. "He changes times and seasons; He deposes kings and raises up others. He gives wisdom to the wise and knowledge to the discerning" (Daniel 2:21). "Whatever the Lord pleases, He does, in heaven and in earth, in the seas and in all deeps. He causes the vapors to ascend from the ends of the earth; Who makes lightnings for the rain? Who brings forth the wind from His treasuries?" (Psalm:135:6-7) "He is before all things, and in Him all things hold together" (Colossians 1:17). Please note that the Scripture did not say that God needs man to help hold anything together. He is God all by Himself.

Who is wiser than God? "Can anyone teach knowledge to God, since He judges even the highest?" (Job 21:22) Who has His power? No one is ahead of God. Man is not greater than His maker. Someone can have a countless number of degrees, however, no one even comes close to God's infinite wisdom and knowledge. Or His power. No one. For those of you who think that you are smarter than God, please repent and humble yourselves. You could be bragging about how much you know one minute, and God could make you forget your name the next minute. Or for the rest of your days, if He wants to.

The earth is God's footstool. That's how mighty and powerful He is. If anything is changing, it's because He wants it to change. And if God wants to change something, there is absolutely nothing that we can do about it. How are humans going to change a climate that we didn't make? Nor can we control the climate. God doesn't need anyone to complete a Census form to know how many people are living on His earth. He knew this information before the foundation of the world. And before He created Adam. Census numbers are inaccurate because not everyone completes a Census form. God is always accurate. He knows the number of hairs on our heads. Talk about precision. As stated earlier, God presides over the world that He, and He alone, created.

Almighty God does not need our help. For anything. And speaking of climate, there is no such thing as Mother Nature. It seems that we always want to give credit to everyone and everything, except God. Mother Nature does not exist, only Father God exists. The Creator of heaven and earth. The great I Am. There is none like Him. "He determines the number of the stars and calls them each by name. Great is our Lord and mighty in power; His understanding has no limit" (Psalm 147:4-5). Instead of focusing on things that do not exist, such as climate change and global warming, we need to take heed to God's global warning — COVID-19.

The persecution of Christians is happening more and more throughout the world. "Yea, and all that will live godly in Christ Jesus shall suffer persecution" (2 Timothy 3:12). In China, they are closing churches, jailing pastors and rewriting Scripture. Whoa unto anyone who tampers with God's Word. "Ye shall not add unto the Word which I command you, neither shall ye diminish ought from it, that ye may keep the commandments of the Lord your God which I command you" (Deuteronomy 4:2).

China concluded another year of unconstitutional and brutal persecutions against believers. North Korea currently leads the world in Christian persecutions. In the Middle East, Christians persecutions are at near genocide levels.

*****

In today's world, we hear a lot about the "rich and powerful." Some people look up to people who are wealthy. It is also what some people aspire to be. Where are all of the millionaires and billionaires of the world? They have all of that money. Can't they do something about COVID-19? Can't they stop this and make it go away? No one could have prevented this from happening. "For the Lord Almighty has purposed, and who can thwart Him? His hand is stretched out, and who can turn it back?" (Isaiah 14:27)

The word powerful often goes hand-in-hand with being rich. But in reality, all human beings are powerless, without God. If any rich man could make COVID-19 go away, they would do so. And quickly.

It's not in their hands. It is not in my hands. It is in the hands of the One who truly has power, the One and Only, Almighty God.

Some rich people today credit themselves for becoming rich. It was their smarts. Their brains. Their this. Their that. It is, God, who made it possible. "Remember the Lord your God, for it is He who gives you the ability to produce wealth, and so confirms His covenant, which He swore to your ancestors, as it is today" (Deuteronomy 8:18). "I say unto you, it is easier for a camel to go through the eye of a needle, than for a rich man to enter into the kingdom of God" (Matthew 19:24). This Bible verse gets misconstrued, often. It does not mean that a rich man cannot go to heaven. There is absolutely nothing wrong with being wealthy or rich. It only becomes a problem if the money becomes your god, which happens often, and it is why Jesus said that. In fact, there were numerous men of God in the Bible, who were rich. Abraham was the Bill Gates of his day. Isaac, Jacob (Israel), David and Job … were all rich men. The one thing that all of these great men of God had in common was that God was first in their lives; they knew Him, honored and worshipped Him. And only Him. They walked in God's statutes and kept His commandments. They also knew that God was their source. For all things. That included their wealth. They messed up sometimes, as we all do. However, whenever they did mess up; they repented.

"Naked I came from my mother's womb, and naked shall I return there. The Lord gave, and the Lord has taken away; blessed be the name of the Lord" (Job 1:21). For those of you who know Job's story, God blessed him with more than he had before going through his trials. It is further proof that God is in control. Of all things.

No matter how rich anyone is, no one is richer than God. In fact, everything belongs to Him. He owns it all. God also controls it all. He can empty any bank account if He chooses to do so, in one fell swoop. There are a number of things that no amount of money can buy. Money can't buy life. It can't buy good health. It can't buy peace of mind. Nor can it buy class. Again, it is fine to have money, as long as it does not have you. "The Lord makes poor and makes rich; He brings low and lifts up" (1 Samuel 2:7). Did anyone notice that the Bible doesn't say that we make ourselves rich?

Some of us are more like another rich and famous man in the Bible, Solomon, David's son. Solomon was very well-known for his wisdom. In fact, when God appeared to Solomon in a dream and asked him what he wanted, Solomon asked for wisdom and knowledge. He didn't ask God for money or material things. Just wisdom and knowledge.

That night God appeared to Solomon and said to him, "Ask for whatever you want Me to give you" (2 Chronicles 7).

Solomon answered God, "You have shown great kindness to David my father and have made me king in his place. Now, Lord God, let your promise to my father David be confirmed, for you have made me king over a people who are as numerous as the dust of the earth. Give me wisdom and knowledge, that I may lead this people, for who is able to govern this great people of yours?" (2 Chronicles 8-10)

God said to Solomon, "Since this is your heart's desire and you have not asked for wealth, possessions or honor, nor for the death of your enemies, and since you have not asked for a long life but for wisdom and knowledge to govern My people over whom I have made you king, therefore wisdom and knowledge will be given you. And I will also give you wealth, possessions and honor, such as no king who was before you ever had and none after you will have" (2 Chronicles 11-12).

Despite all that God had given Solomon, when he became old, his multiple wives turned his heart after other gods. He turned away from the One True God and started worshipping false gods. The Bible tells us that Solomon's heart was not fully devoted to God as his father David's had been. David had a passionate love for God. He was a man after God's own heart. Note, after God's heart, not after more riches or material things. So, while David had wealth, his wealth did not have him. Like Solomon, some of us have also turned to gods.

There were great men and women of God in the Bible. Were any of them perfect? Absolutely not. They were very flawed like you and me. For example, the man who was after God's own heart, David, committed adultery and impregnated a married woman.

And if that wasn't bad enough, he had that same woman's husband killed, because he wanted his beautiful wife. Sounds similar to today's must-see soap operas. The baby didn't live. This is also the same David, who as a boy, killed the giant, Goliath, with God's help. When David did sin, he prayed and repented. He would also fast sometimes.

Arguably the greatest prophet in the Bible, Moses, killed someone. Saul, whose name was changed to Paul by God, persecuted Christians. In addition to murderers and adulterers, there were also liars. Some also struggled with faith and doubted God, (sound familiar)? God still used these men. This should be very encouraging for you and me. In fact, it should give us hope. The only perfect One in the Bible was Jesus.

Thank God that He is forgiving and merciful. Thank God for His grace. Where would we be without it? But most importantly, where would we be without God's unsurpassed love for us? God knows that we are not perfect. He also knows that we will mess up sometimes. There is no such thing as a small sin, a medium-sized sin or a big sin. In God's eyes, sin is sin. There is no shade of gray. When we sin, we need to ask God for forgiveness and repent.

*****

COVID-19 happened because we did what Israel did, time and time again, we turned away from God and started worshipping other gods: money, material things, celebrities, our careers ... This global pandemic is what can happen when the world rejects its Creator. Sin *is* the root cause of COVID-19. If we are not wise, if we don't take heed to God's global warning, He could do something much worse.

God is long-suffering. He is slow to anger. This is the year 2020. For years and years, God watched as we rejected Him. He has watched as we became more arrogant. More prideful. He has watched while He blessed us and we thanked everyone, but Him. We exist to serve God. To glorify Him and worship Him. In spirit and in truth.

The One and Only All-Powerful God does not need us. We need Him. "God that made the world and all things therein, seeing that He is Lord of heaven and earth, dwelleth not in temples made with hands; neither is worshipped with men's hands, as though He needed anything, seeing He giveth to all life, and breath, and all things ..." (Acts 17 24:25). We are all in God's hands. COVID-19 is also in His hands. Only God can remove COVID-19 from His world.

Many of us are beyond stressed out. Some of us are also very scared. In order to have peace, we must know Jesus and seek Him. And if God ends this global pandemic, we need to thank Him.

God loves us. He sent His Son, Jesus, to die on the cross for us. "For God so loved the world that He gave His only begotten Son, that whoever believes in Him shall not perish but have everlasting life" (John 3:16).

Where do we go from here? Many of you may be saying, "back to work! That's where I need to go."

What is God's message to us? From God's own words, we need to turn back to Him and repent. This worldwide shutdown is, and should be, a time of self-reflection. For each of us. We have all sinned and fallen short of the glory of God. Yes, millions need and want to get back to work. Yes, we want the world to go back to the way we once knew it. And, yes, we want to get out of the house and do all of the things that we love doing. However, the first thing we need to do is repent and turn back to God. Worship Him and glorify Him. And thank Him for His many blessings. Thank Him in good times and in bad times. We must go from no Jesus to know Jesus. Instead of focusing on "getting back to normal," we need to focus on, "getting back to God."

In the midst of suffering, whether it be a global pandemic, an accident, or a sick loved one, we know that God is not pleased with the perishing of people but desires all people to come to salvation. Even though God does not desire our perishing, He uses suffering to bring people to salvation. "And we know that in all things God works for the good of those who love Him, who have been called according to His purpose" (Romans 8:28). His purpose. Not ours.

If this global pandemic does not remind us that God is in control, and we are not, few things will. Turning away from God got us here. Therefore, humbling ourselves, repenting and turning back to God, will help get us out.

"When I shut up the heavens so that there is no rain, or command locusts to devour the land or send a plague among my people; If My people, who are called by My name, will humble themselves and pray and seek My face and turn from their wicked ways, then I will hear from heaven, and I will forgive their sin and will heal their land" (Chronicles 7:13-14).

In a world full of darkness, we need to turn to the Son. The vaccine that **the world needs**, most, is **a biblical vaccine.** The name that is above *every* name — **JESUS.**

****

SCRIPTURES ON FEAR

"Prayer, minus worry, equals faith in God." ™

~Michelle Cole

"When I am afraid, I put my trust in You" (Psalm 56:3).

"Who of you by worrying can add a single hour to his life?" (Matthew 6:27)

"The Lord is my light and my salvation — whom shall I fear? The Lord is the stronghold of my life — of whom shall I be afraid?" (Psalm 27:1)

"Have I not commanded you? Be strong and courageous. Do not be afraid; do not be discouraged, for the Lord your God will be with you wherever you go" (Joshua 1:9).

"For God hath not given us the spirit of fear; but of power, and of love, and of a sound mind" (2 Timothy 1:7).

He got up, rebuked the wind and said to the waves, "Peace! Be still!" Then the wind died down and it was completely calm. He said to His disciples, "Why are you so afraid? O ye of little faith?" (Mark 4:39-40)

"I sought the Lord, and He answered me; He delivered me from all my fears" (Psalm 34:4).

"Therefore do not worry about tomorrow, for tomorrow will worry about itself. Each day has enough trouble of its own" (Matthew 6:34).

SCRIPTURES ON GOD'S OMNIPOTENCE

"For by Him all things were created, in heaven and on earth, visible and invisible, whether thrones or dominions or rulers or authorities — all things were created through Him and for Him" (Colossians 1:16).

"Who knoweth not in all these that the hand of the LORD hath wrought this? In whose hand is the soul of every living thing, and the breath of all mankind" (Job 12:9-10).

God declares the end from the beginning. "I am the Alpha and the Omega" says the Lord God, "who is and was and is to come the Almighty" (Revelation 1:8).

"He gives life, and He brings death; He wounds and He heals" (Deuteronomy 32:39).

"Nothing has happened in the world that God has not commanded, both good and bad" (Lamentations 3:37-38).

"All the inhabitants of the earth are accounted as nothing, But He does according to His will in the host of heaven And among the inhabitants of earth; And no one can ward off His hand Or say to Him," 'What have You done?' (Daniel 4:35)

"His counsel will stand, and no purpose of His can be thwarted" (Isaiah 46:10, Job 42:2).

"He alone is the God over all creation" (Psalm 103:19).

SCRIPTURES ON HEALING

But He was wounded for our transgressions, crushed for our iniquities; upon Him was the punishment that made us whole, and by His stripes we are healed (Isaiah 53:4-6).

"Behold, I am the Lord, the God of all flesh, is there anything too hard for Me?" (Jeremiah 32:27)

"Heal me, O Lord, and I shall be healed; save me, and I shall be saved; for You are my praise" (Jeremiah 17:14).

"A cheerful heart is good medicine, but a crushed spirit dries up the bones" (Proverbs 17:22).

"Worship the Lord your God, and His blessing will be on your food and water. I will take away sickness from among you" (Exodus 23:25).

When Jesus entered Peter's house, He saw his mother-in-law lying in bed with a fever; He touched her hand, and the fever left her, and she got up and began to serve Him (Matthew 8:14–15).

And straightway the fountain of her blood was dried up; and she felt in her body that she was healed of that plague. And Jesus, immediately knowing in Himself that virtue had gone out of Him, turned Him about in the press, and said, "Who touched My clothes?" And His disciples said unto Him, "Thou seest the multitude thronging thee, and sayest Thou, who touched Me?" (Mark 5:29-31)

WHAT MUST I DO TO BE SAVED?

"Dear Lord Jesus, I know that I am a sinner, and I ask for Your forgiveness. Jesus, I believe You died for my sins and rose from the dead. I turn from my sins and invite You to come into my heart and life. I want to trust and follow You as my Lord and Savior."

**ACTS 2:37-41:

Now when they heard this, they were pricked in their heart, and said unto Peter and to the rest of the apostles, "Men and brethren, what shall we do?"

Then Peter said unto them, "Repent, and be baptized every one of you in the name of Jesus Christ for the remission of sins, and ye shall receive the gift of the Holy Ghost."

"For the promise is unto you, and to your children, and to all that are afar off, even as many as the LORD our God shall call."

And with many other words did he testify and exhort, saying, "Save yourselves from this untoward generation."

Then they that gladly received His Word were baptized: and the same day there were added unto them about three thousand souls.

Dear Readers:

I hope that you enjoyed reading this book as much as I enjoyed writing it.

Be Blessed!

~Michelle Cole

www.ingramcontent.com/pod-product-compliance
Lightning Source LLC
Chambersburg PA
CBHW060623030426
42337CB00018B/3157